Lake Minnewanka

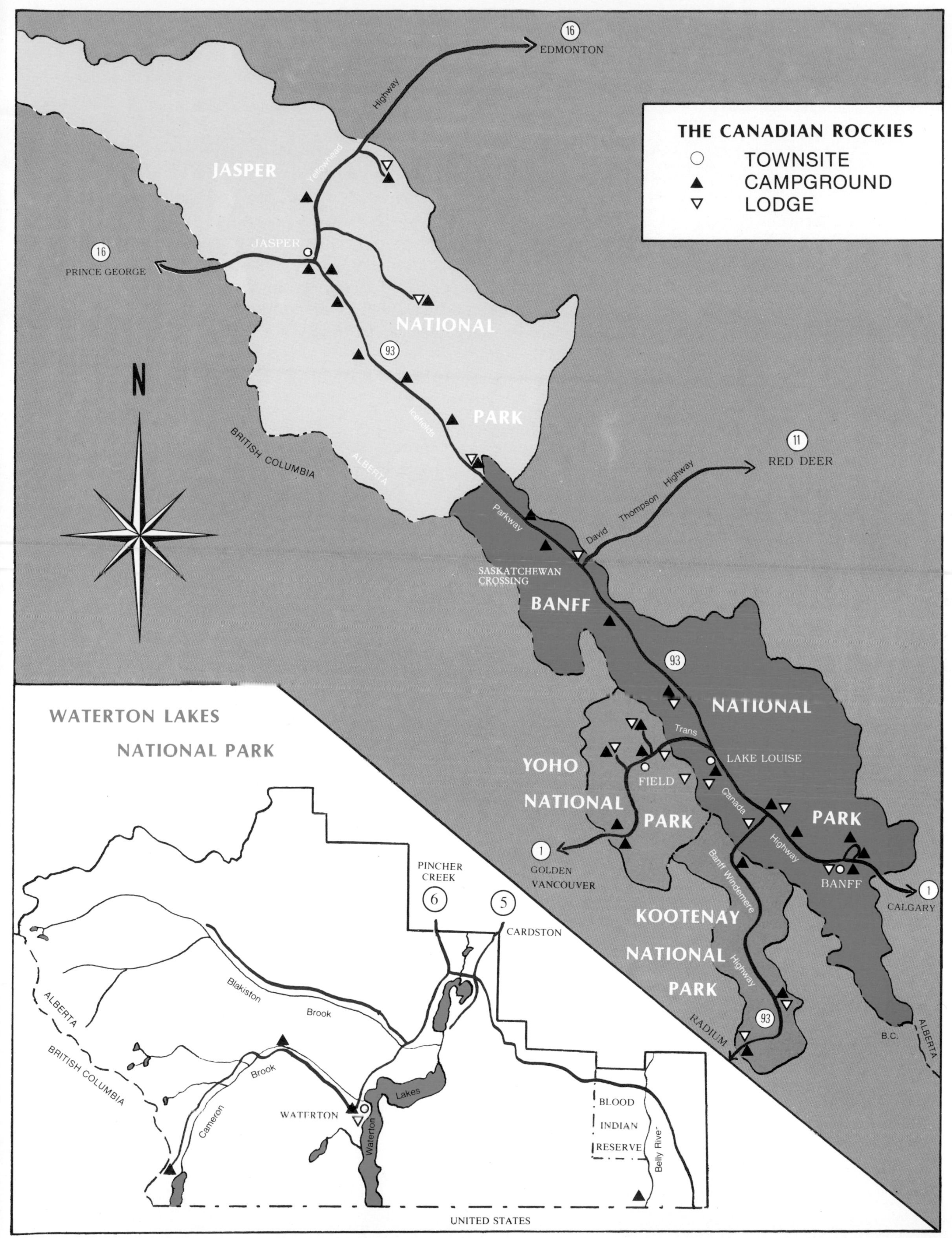
THE CANADIAN ROCKIES
TOWNSITE
CAMPGROUND
LODGE
16
EDMONTON
Yellowhead
Highway
JASPER
JASPER
16
PRINCE GEORGE
NATIONAL
93
Icefields
PARK
BRITISH COLUMBIA
ALBERTA
11
RED DEER
David
Thompson
Highway
Parkway
SASKATCHEWAN CROSSING
BANFF
93
NATIONAL
Trans
LAKE LOUISE
YOHO
FIELD
NATIONAL
Canada
PARK
PARK
Highway
1
GOLDEN
VANCOUVER
Banff Windemere
BANFF
1
CALGARY
KOOTENAY
NATIONAL
Highway
PARK
93
RADIUM
B.C.
ALBERTA
WATERTON LAKES
NATIONAL PARK
PINCHER CREEK
6
5
CARDSTON
ALBERTA
Blakiston
Brook
BRITISH COLUMBIA
Brook
Cameron
Lakes
WATERTON
Waterton
BLOOD
INDIAN
RESERVE
Belly River
UNITED STATES

THE CANADIAN ROCKIES

Mother Nature's monolithic self-portrait of merciless strength and fragile beauty. Of this landscape, more than any, is she most vulnerable to the ignorance and the envy of Man. To more greatly appreciate and respect her resources we must think of Nature in terms of ourselves.

What we call the Elements are qualities possessed in forming of her character. The seasons by which she exhibits these adds to them personality. Thoreau saw nature in this very manner. The lake he saw as the earth's eye and the trees next the shore its slender eyelashes. Are autumn Aspens not then her golden hair? And the multitude of colourful wildflowers adorning the alpine meadows only enhance her beauty-like cosmetics, I fain say.

It is with these images in mind that we should behold Nature, for to preserve, protect and admire her forever.

With this very intention the Canadian government, in 1885, designated a Federal Reserve of ten square miles around a mineral hot spring near present-day Banff townsite. That decision initiated our National Parks system, which today encompasses more than 20,000 square kilometers throughout the Canadian Rockies. This area is made of five separate parks: Banff, Jasper, Kootenay, Yoho and Waterton Lakes.

The parks exhibit what is a true Natural History Museum, attracting millions of visitors each year. This pictorial guide shows to you some of the most beautiful and famous scenes witnessed while passing along the parks' roadways.

And there is so much to do . . . Imagination and enthusiasm allows the visitor to participate in a host of recreational activities.

■ HIKING is what the mountains are all about; to escape society so as to find yourself, or lose yourself, in silent contemplation. Bring along a camera; to reminisce over photographs of wildflowers and wildlife, lofty peaks and emerald lakes, makes a memory all the warmer. Bookshops at the townsites will sell you a comprehensive Trail Guide. Choosing from thousands of kilometres of trail, there are short, simple day-hikes or vigorous, week-long expeditions.

■ CAMPING is available in the parks at designated areas only. There are campsites next the roadways, near the townsites and in the backcountry. Campsites, for the most, are open from mid-May to October, but there is likewise winter camping permitted in each park. A list of available campgrounds accompanies the chapter to the individual parks. For more information as to campground locations, fees, etc., visit an Information Bureau in any of the parks. Fires are to be made only in the fireplaces provided. It is necessary, however, to carry a small campstove to the primitive, backcountry campsites.

■ FISHING permits must be obtained from a Park Information Bureau. While you're there, if need be, inquire as to the best stocked lakes and streams, or hire a guide. Local residents won't disclose their favorite fishing holes — they'll sooner lead you astray. Common species include Dolly Varden, whitefish, cutthroat and several trouts.

■ BOATING by oar, canoe or kayak may be exercised on most rivers and lakes. Power boats are restricted to Lake Minnewanka in Banff Park, to Lakes Pyramid and Medicine in Jasper Park, and to Upper Waterton Lake in Waterton Lakes Park.

Bow Lake

■ CLIMBING is becoming a more popular pastime each year. Many professional climbers use the Canadian Rockies as their training ground. If you're intent on this hazardous activity, climbing guides are available to you. Good luck! and I suggest you register your destination with the Park Warden Office.

■ SKIING downhill in the Canadian Rockies is of the best in North America. Also, hundreds upon hundreds of kilometres of trail are accessible to the cross-country skier.

GEOLOGY

Components of sandstone, siltstone, limestone, dolomite, quartzite and shale can be discerned from the Rocky Mountains. These rock types, having eventually filled an entire inland sea, were formed in layers thousands of feet thick by an accumulation of sands, silts, clays and mud. It is believed that much of this rock is some 600 million years old.

Several hundred million years passed when great forces beneath the earth's crust, together with the influential weight of the ocean encroaching upon the continental shelf, persuaded these enormous layers of rock to uplift, bend and fold - creating above the earth's surface a mountainous terrain.

57 million years ago the monoliths were made.

From that time, until as recently as 10,000 years ago, at least four major Ice Ages occurred. Climatic changes allowed glaciers to maintain themselves and further grow to a thickness of several thousand feet, covering all but the highest of peaks. At the decline of each Ice Age, as the glaciers retreated (slowly melted), they left in their wake deep U-shaped valleys with high cliff-like walls. Fine examples of these valleys now contain such river systems as the Athabasca, the Bow and the North Saskatchewan. And as the glaciers advance and retreat they, with flowing water, wind and rain, sculpt and carve the rock into the most peculiar shapes. The debris from this erosion collects along the lower slopes of mountains. These are moraines. The yet finer debris — sand, silt, clay, et cetra — is carried by the water through the river systems, back to sea level; deposited there as sedimentary rock, it enables nature to make mountains out of mud.

VEGETATION

Plant life in the Canadian Rockies is divided into three ecological zones. Waterton Lakes, from the other four National Parks, differs only slightly in its vegetation. Greater detail is given to this in the chapter on Waterton Lakes.

The MONTANE ZONE occupies the low valleys and to an elevation of about 4,800 feet (1,460 metres) yet it can sometimes be detected at 5,000 ft. (1,520 metres) on south-facing slopes. Growing here are such trees as cottonwood and aspen poplars, lodgepole and limber pines, douglas fir and white spruce.

The SUBALPINE ZONE extends from the montane to the timberline at 7,200 ft. (2,200 metres) with dominant species of Englemann spruce and alpine fir. Other trees include lodgepole pine, alpine larch and whitebark pine.

Interspersed within the montane and subalpine zones are many shrubs and berries (some species being edible), and in the meadows — wildflowers!

The ALPINE ZONE — above timberline — with its strong winds and cold temperatures, has a growing season of about 60 days — unable to sustain life for all but a few shrubs and grasses.

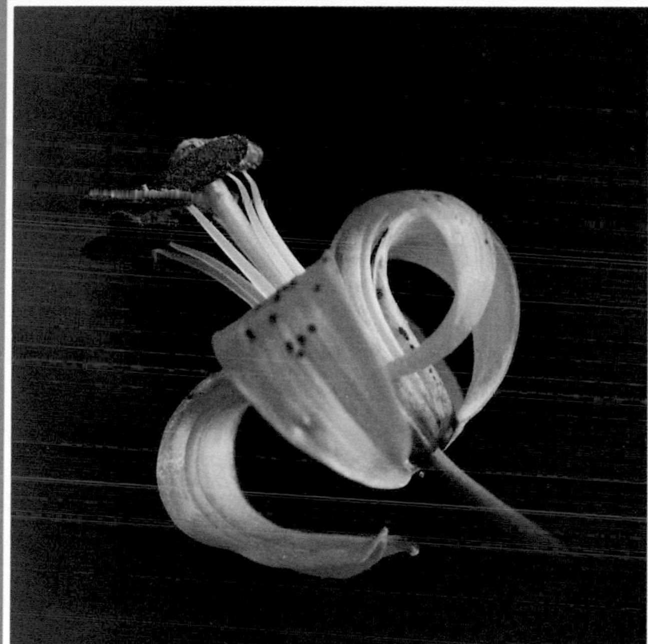

WILDLIFE

The great expectation of most visitors to the Canadian Rockies is to observe the wildlife. Some animals are less frequently observed than others. This is due, infact, as I have mentioned, to man's ignorance — having caused so many species to become rare and endangered. The National Parks are a sanctuary for wildlife, perhaps the last refuge to protect them from extinction.

PIKA — about 6 inches (15 cm.) long with grey fur, mouse-like face, small round ears and no distinguishable tail — lives in rockslides at timberline and on alpine slopes.

PACK RAT — similar in size to the Pika, it has long ears and a long, bushy stiff tail — lives also in rockslides and inhabits the Alpine Huts — also known as "Traders", they have a mania to collect objects for their nest, only to replace them with a pebble or twig.

SNOWSHOE RABBIT — lives in dense forests throughout the subalpine — in winter changes colour from brown to white.

CHIPMUNKS are only 4 inches (10 cm.) long with an erect tail, and stripes the entire length of the body and head — live in logs and rockslides in the montane and subalpine.

GOLDEN-MANTLED GROUND SQUIRREL — somewhat larger than the Chipmunk, but its stripes do not mark the head — also inhabits areas similar to the Chipmunk.

COLUMBIAN GROUND SQUIRREL — more often seen then the Golden-mantled or Chipmunk, they burrow in colonies in grasslands and meadows — with mottled grey fur, they stand 12 inches (30 cm.) upon their hind legs.

RED SQUIRREL — about 8 inches (20 cm.) long with reddish fur and a long bushy tail — known for their consistent chattering, they inhabit spruce and pine trees within the montane and subalpine forests.

HOARY MARMOT — can be 20 inches (50 cm.) long and weigh 20 lbs. (9 kilos) brown coloured with a large, flat tail (similar to the beaver's, only fur-covered) — known for their "whistle"-noise, they inhabit rockslides at and above timberline.

PORCUPINE — about the size and weight of a Marmot, they inhabit subalpine forests nocturnally — they move very slowly and are entirely covered with long, sharp quills which they do not throw; quills are released upon contact with objects.

BEAVER — having dark brown, water-repellent fur, a large, flat leathery tail, they inhabit ponds, streams and marshlands at low elevation. Their protruding front teeth gnaw through trees; trees and branches being used to build their "dam"-houses. The Beaver may be 30 inches (75 cm.) long weighing sometimes 55 lbs. (25 kilos).

COYOTE — a medium-sized dog with a slender muzzle and bushy tail. Their nocturnal howl is distinctive, yet they are also active during daylight, feeding on ground squirrels and mice. They are prey for larger carnivores such as wolves, cougars and bears.

BIGHORN SHEEP — the male is distinguished by large curled horns. They are brownish coloured, except for the white rump. Adults can weight 300 lbs. (135 kilos). They are very sure-footed, usually inhabiting open slopes, but may venture to rock cliffs to escape predators.

MOUNTAIN GOAT — they are seldom seem. Being more sure-footed than sheep they inhabit extremely high, seemingly inaccessible cliffs. Both male and female have pointed black horns and thick, white coats.

MULE DEER — so called for its mule-like ears. Their colour varies from reddish-brown to grey, with black being noticed on the tip of the short tail. They can weight 400 lbs. (180 kilos), and the males possess antlers which they lose each midwinter.

Grizzly Bear

Mountain Goat

Otter

ELK — also known as Wapiti, they weight up to 1,000 lbs. (450 kilos), have a pale rump and a reddish-brown coat which is darker about the legs and neck than on the torso. The males have huge antlers which they lose in late winter or early spring. Elk inhabit the montane valleys, and Banff and Jasper golf course most of the year.

MOOSE — the largest of the deer family, weighing as much as 1,100 lbs. (500 kilos) and wearing enormous palmate antlers by the male. They have humped shoulders and a dewlap hangs from the throat. Moose inhabit the valleys, shallow lakes and marshland.

BLACK BEAR — they are not necessarily black, but may be brown, cinnamon or blonde. The black bear has a pointed face and lacks the humped shoulders of the grizzly. Weighing up to 500 lbs. (225 kilos), these omnivores inhabit the mountain valleys and subalpine forests. Black bears can climb trees.

GRIZZLY BEAR — larger than the black bear — 800 lbs. (360 kilos), with a flat, broad face and large shoulder humps. Colouration is similar to the black bear. Grizzlies have poor eyesight but a great sense of smell. This solitary omnivore will usually inhabit backcountry meadows, avoiding man wherever possible.

Black Bear

Elk

Bighorn Sheep

EXPLORATION, DISCOVERY AND SETTLEMENT

Indians — Blackfoot, Cree, Stoney, Kootenay — had known these "Shining Mountains" for many generations before a Hudson's Bay Company employee first beheld this landscape in the mid 18th century.

By the turn of the next century fur traders from Upper and Lower Canadas were seeking passages through the Rockies in search, ultimately, of the Pacific Ocean. Hence began a rivalry between the North West Company and the Hudson's Bay Company at establishing trading posts throughout the lucrative land.

In 1807, David Thompson, trader and surveyor with the North West Company, initiated human settlement when, by crossing present-day Howse Pass, he penetrated into unmapped country and constructed a trade post in the Columbia Valley. Piegan Indians deterred further gain, forcing Thompson to seek an alternative route to the Pacific. This adventure, in 1811, let to his discovery of the Athabasca Pass, consequently establishing Henry's House near present-day Jasper townsite. Another post — Jasper's House — was built east of here one year later.

Slowly but surely explorations gained a momentum. By 1825, naturalists like Thomas Drummond, for example, and the botanist, David Douglas, were conducting detailed studies. What next? Geologists, surveyors, mountaineers! A painter and preacher! Man's enthusiasm and determination, to say the least!

Hudson's Bay Governor Sir George Simpson — wasn't he reliable in the eyes of the British Government? After all, he did commission Paul Kane to produce 12 paintings. But no!, he hadn't shown positive results. It was as though, what with newly discovered land, one could simply go about naming places for himself and leave it at that!

1857. British Columbia is now a crown colony. We need to unite British Columbia with the east..Get rid of Simpson! Get me...get me Captain John Palliser and Dr. James Hector! Survey the mountains with the objective to construct roads and railways.

The Captain and his geologist separated. Palliser discovered Kananaskis. And Hector — he camped beside the Bow River on a "beautiful small prairie" (later to become Banff's townsite), awakened the following morning to climb and name Castle Mountain. He then discovered Vermilion Pass and then yet another . . . crossing a turbulent river, his horse kicks him. Kicking Horse Pass! Isn't history peculiar!

He then adventured along the North Saskatchewan River before the Palliser Expedition concluded its surveys. Yes, it was possible to construct roads and railways.

Sir Sandford Fleming, Engineer-in-Chief with the Canadian Pacific Railway in 1872 — surveyed and chose the Yellowhead Pass as the route for the railroad through the Rockies, but this idea was rejected as it was too far north; so, in 1881, Major A.B. Rogers surveyed the Bow Valley-Kicking Horse Pass and decided it more economical. This proposal was accepted, thus allowing William Cornelius Van Horne, with his Chinese and European labourers, to commence work. By 1885 the railroad was completed and the country united.

During the rail construction surveyors were likewise making discoveries. Silver City flourished as a town dependent on its copper and silver. Unfortunately, its resources were quickly depleted. It existed for two short years (1883-1885) on a meadow between present-day Banff and Johnston's Canyon.

Anthracite was a coal mining town established near Johnston Lake in 1886. It was likewise short lived (until 1904) when a new, larger coal mining town began nearby.

Bankhead, between Banff townsite and Lake Minnewanka, pulsated until 1923; the economy took a turn for the worse, as it were, depriving its 1,000 residents.

Other settlements saw a different fate....

Another discovery! — that of Lake Louise in 1882 by Tom Wilson — saw the CPR build a station at nearby Laggan (today's Lake Louise Village). They built yet another — Field, 1884 — and within two years the CPR constructed their first hotel, Mount Stephen House, at this site.

Hot mineral springs are discovered at Sulphur Mountain in 1885 and the federal government reserves ten square miles surrounding them. This introduces Canada to a National Park system. The government continues to create: in 1887 they enlarge the area at Banff to 260 square miles and name it Rocky Mountains National Park.

Meanwhile, Van Horne is building another hotel, the Banff Springs, with the intention to advertise the Canadian Rockies as a vacation playground. Tourism is born.

At Field, Mount Stephen House is bustling with tourism so the government reserves

Postcard, Valentine and Sons

Mount Stephen House, Field, B.C., on Canadian Pacific Railway

Lake Louise Hotel, Laggan, Canadian Rockies

ten square miles (1886). Yoho stood as such until 1901 when it was expanded to cover an area of 828 square miles.

The CPR leaves its mark once more by accommodating people in a chalet on the shore to Lake Louise (1890).

In the southern reaches of the Canadian Rockies, nearing the U.S. border — a region surveyed in 1859 by the Palliser Expedition — came the discovery of oil. 1895 was the year in which was established the 54 square miles of Waterton Lakes National Park.

In the northern Rockies there would eventually be constructed another railroad. The Yellowhead Pass was its likely course. Thus, in 1907, Jasper National Park was established in anticipation of the event. And sure enough! four years later a train rolls along the tracks of the Grand Trunk Pacific Railway and stops at the station at Fitzhugh. The town is renamed as Jasper two years later.

Then for some reason — heaven knows why! — the Canadian Northern Railway lays their tracks parallel to the Grand Trunk. Where's the logic?, especially when in the same year (1915) the government lifted its restrictions on the use of automobiles. The road from Banff to Lake Louise was completed in 1920. A road through the Vermilion Pass in

The Banff Springs Hotel

1923 brought about the establishment of Kootenay National Park — for to preserve the natural phenomena on either side of the Banff-Windermere Highway.

There is now, for the most part, an efficient and convenient system of railways and roadways through the mountains, yet there remains one route that may only be journeyed with horses. Perhaps the most beautiful of North American landscapes, abundant with rivers, lakes and glaciers, is the trail from Banff to Jasper. It took ten years to construct the Banff-Jasper Highway. Since its opening in 1940, the National Parks of the Canadian Rockies appear as they were then and shall always be; that of a natural wonder beheld by all who visit or make it their home.

UPPER SPRINGS. BANFF. CANADIAN ROCKIES.

BUFFALO. ROCKY MT. PARK. BANFF.

Banff Springs Hotel

Banff townsite at night from Mt. Norquay

Castle Mountain

BANFF NATIONAL PARK

By 1883, the Canadian Pacific Railway had reached westward to the Rockies. As the tracks came through the Bow Valley past present-day Banff Townsite, two of the employees happened to discover a hot mineral spring on the north slope of nearby Sulphur Mountain. The government, rather than recognize a claim to the pools by the two men, designated an area of ten square miles around the Cave and Basin Springs as a Federal Reserve. That decision in 1885 created Canada's first National Park.

Now the CPR, having driven the last spike in 1885, wished to capitalize on the scenery as a potential tourist attraction. So, in 1886, they began construction of a few resort hotels in the Rockies; one of which was the Banff Springs, a stone's throw from the hot pools.

A year later, the government enlarged their Reserve to 260 square miles. The park of 1887 was named Rocky Mountains National Park.

Such a hotel as large and luxurious as the Banff Springs would surely have great demands...enough to cause a town to emerge across the river! Shops, houses, restaurants, a transport company to conduct scenic excursions. The CPR went so far as to import their own genuine Swiss alpinists. The people weren't about to sit in musty hotel rooms all day — not with all that wilderness! The mountaineers — incidentally, having imported their architecture as well — would guide the tourist to the top of the highest mountain, besides offer the town a rather eccentric reputation. The busy little alpine village was named Banff; CPR President Lord Mount (George) Stephen was a native of Banffshire, Scotland.

The town was growing. Paved roads led a destiny to Lake Louise in 1920. The National Parks Act of 1930 draughted new boundaries at 2,564 square miles (6,641 sq. km.), renaming the reserve as Banff National Park.

Today's Banff portrays a dual personality. It is at once a cosmopolitan resort, accommodating millions of visitors from the four corners of the globe; and yet it retains the comfortable size and intimate charm of a small mountain town, where any of the 4,500 inhabitants may escape the rat—race for the pleasures of nature in a matter of minutes.

Besides the infamous Banff Springs Hotel, with its many dining-rooms, shops, swimming pools and picturesque golf course, there are within the townsite numerous smaller, less expensive hotels and motels to choose as lodgings.

Those hungry for knowledge will find the Peter and Catharine Whyte Foundation of particular interest. The building houses the Archives of the Canadian Rockies, its shelves bloated with priceless publications for mountaineers and naturalists.

On the west slope of Tunnel Mountain, facing the townsite, is the world renowned Banff Centre for Continuing Education, where studies in the Fine Arts are undertaken in a most creative environment.

Banff also has three museums. The Natural History Museum in the Clock Tower Mall has rocks and fossils for the geological enthusiast. The Park Museum, across the street in the public park, displays a taxidermic collection of wildlife, fishes, birds and insects. The Luxton Museum is a replica of a fur trader's fort; inside of which one may discover the early fur trade and the Indian cultures of the Rocky Mountains.

Hiking trails, fishing holes, campsites are all within reach of the townsite. Information and interpretive services are available at the Parks Canada Information Bureau on Banff Avenue.

Banff townsite and the Bow Valley may be observed from either of two easily accessible viewpoints. Sulphur Mountain, with its Upper Hot Springs, has a Gondola to lift you to the teahouse and observation deck at the summit. Looking east from the summit is a striking pose made by Mount Rundle (2949 m). The other viewpoint is from Mount Norquay, reached from the town's west exit. From the parking lot of the ski hill is a good look at Cascade Mountain (2998 m).

North of Banff townsite is the road to Lake Minnewanka. Passing the ruins of the Bankhead, an early coal mining town, one arrives at the shores of the deep, glacier-fed lake. The lake, below the cliffs of Mount Inglismaldie (2964 m), is a favoured spot for sailing, windsurfing and motor boats. The road continues toward Two Jack Lake, a lovely setting for the canoeist and fisherman. A third, much smaller lake, Johnston Lake, is discovered as a comfortable place to fish, bathe and picnic.

The Trans-Canada heads west from Banff, past the junction to Sunshine Village ski area, toward Lake Louise and, eventually, through Yoho National Park. An alternative route to this congested highway is the Bow Valley Parkway, intersecting the Trans-Canada just west of Banff townsite. This scenic drive through the Bow Valley, alongside the Bow River and the CPR, leads to the much visited attraction of Johnston Canyon. A self-guiding trail follows the steep, narrow gorges of Johnston Canyon. The Upper and Lower Falls create the rushing waters which erode the limestone walls.

On approaching the unmistakable Castle Mountain (2766 m) there is a main junction with the parkway. The road leads westward, intersects with the Trans-Canada Highway, and continues as the Banff-Windermere Highway into Kootenay National Park.

The Bow Valley Parkway ultimately leads to the most celebrated natural wonder of the Canadian Rockies — Lake Louise. The Indians guided Tom Wilson of the CPR to their "lake of little fishes" in 1882. He named the amazing discovery of Emerald Lake, for its colour truly is of this precious gemstone — but the Royal Geographic Society soon changed the name to honour the Governor General's Wife Princess Louise Caroline Alberta.

And it took no time whatsoever for the CPR to capitalize on Wilsons's discovery. By 1890 they had built a Chalet on the shore of Lake Louise. The Chalet greatly encouraged tourism, scientific exploration and mountaineering expeditions. The fantastic collage of rugged peaks and glaciers encompassing the peaceful lake was soon exploited to sad proportions. Man moved in without invitation and took over...The New Chateau Lake Louise, built after the fire of 1924, sits in the same place as the old Chalet, looking onto the unconsciously disturbed lake and the nervous, ever-grumbling glacier on Mount Victoria (3464 m). The many hikes and climbs in the area offer countless views of the reality which a painter's brush shall never successfully imitiate.

While you're this high on the mountains, you might as well get your money's worth, so to speak. A short drive of 14 kilometres reveals the infamous scene on the Canadian 20 dollar bill — Moraine Lake and the Valley of the Ten Peaks. Magnanimous to the mind, the ten peaks of the Wenkchemna Range rise majestically above the still, blue water of Moraine Lake. Here, as at Lake Louise, hikes and climbs offer views that will take your breath away.

The Lake Louise Ski Area — North America's finest — is located on the north side of the Bow Valley from Village Lake Louise.

The Trans-Canada, less than three kilometres later, intersects with the Icefields Parkway. The Trans-Canada continues west into Yoho National Park via the Kicking Horse Pass. The Icefields Parkway — one of life's most scenic excursions — follows the Continental Divide through the northwest of Banff National Park where it eventually meets the boundary with Jasper National Park.

What constitutes the Parkway's reputation? See for yourself! Lake after shimmery lake; river after riotous river; waterfalls upon waterfalls; seemingly endless ranges of monolithic mountains and creeping, crawling glaciers; meadows colourfully costumed with wildflowers dancing in the wind, and dark, intimidating forests alive with the multilingual utterance of mother nature; the dreamy flight of a solitary golden eagle in the light of the life-giving sunshine. Wouldn't you vote for such a constitution?

The Parkway begins by following the Bow River past Herbert Lake and Hector Lake. Mount Hector (3394 m) and its glacial companion stands solemnly to the east. To the west suddenly appears the massive Crowfoot Glacier, hanging above Bow Lake between Bow Peak (2868 m) and Crowfoot Mountain.

A hike around the emerald waters of Bow Lake leads to Bow Falls. The Bow Glacier, part of the Wapta Icefield, is the source of the Bow River.

Passing over the Bow Summit (2069 m) toward Peyto Lake, the river systems take on a new direction. All waters between this apex and the Saskatchewan Glacier of the Columbia Icefield flow into the North Saskatchewan River System, whereas the Bow River Flows into the South Saskatchewan River.

From the observation deck above Peyto Lake, also fed by the Wapta Icefield, one stares hypnotically at the still, turquois waters. The beauty of this lake appears convincingly unreal to many people. A hike to the shores of Peyto Lake passes through the damp mystical forest, filled with strangely colourful mushrooms and wildflowers.

The Parkway now follows the Mistaya River, fed by Peyto Lake, past numerous other lakes just as beautiful in the eye of the beholder.

The Mistaya and North Saskatchewan Rivers meet at the point where David Thompson first crossed the Rockies in 1807. The North Saskatchewan River originates from the Saskatchewan Glacier of the Columbia Icefields.

At the Saskatchewan River Crossing is the junction with the David Thompson Highway, leading east along the river toward Red Deer on the Alberta prairies. A trail west follows the Howse River to Howse Pass.

The Parkway Lodge, with a spectacular view of Mount Wilson (3240 m) and Mount Murchison (3333 m) is a perfect place to enjoy a meal and a rest, or to gather information for the journey farther into the Canadian Rockies.

Tents and recreational vehicles are accommodated from either May or June until mid-September at the following areas: Castle Mountain, Cirrus Mountain, Johnson's Canyon, Lake Louise, Mosquito Creek, Protection Mountain, Rampart Creek, Two Jack Lake, Tunnel Mountain, Waterfowl Lake.

Winter camping is provided at Lake Louise, Mosquito Creek and Tunnel Mountain.

For information, contact the Superintendent, Banff National Park, Box 900, Banff, Alberta TOL OCO. Telephone (403) 762-3324.

Lake Louise

The Chateau and Lake Louise

Sulphur Mountain Gondola

Abbot Hut

opposite: Mt. Chephren and Waterfowl Lakes.

Crowfoot Glacier

Bow Lake

opposite: Bow Falls, Bow Lake

Peyto Lake

Mount Saskatchewan

opposite: Athabasca Falls

JASPER NATIONAL PARK

Jasper is the largest National Park in the Canadian Rockies — 10,878 sq. km — and the second largest reserve in North America.

This immense landscape portrays itself today in very much the same vein it did to the fur traders and explorers 150 years ago. In having constructed a highway from Banff to Jasper townsite — commenced in 1931, completed in 1940 — the Icefields Parkway gives easy access to so many a scenic viewpoint and to some 1,000 km of backcountry hiking and cross-country skiing. The Icefields Parkway, the length of which measures 230 km, stretches in a northwest direction, following the Bow, Mistaya, North Saskatchewan, Sunwapta and Athabasca Rivers along the east side of the Great Divide.

Entering Jasper National Park from the south, from Banff Park, the boundary is recognized via Sunwapta Pass (2035 m). Here is the first of several excellent views of Mount Athabasca (3491 m). Within a few minutes, you arrive at the Columbia Icefield Chalet, providing accommodations, food, and gasoline.

The Columbia Icefield is a massive sheet of thick glacial ice, encompassing an area of 389 sq. km atop the Great Divide. Of the several large glaciers fed by the Icefield, the Athabasca Glacier displays itself most prominently. It flows to a length of 7 km toward the Chalet between Mount Athabasca and Mount Kitchener (3475 m). To the left of here is the Dome Glacier and Mount Snowdome, a geographical phenomenon. From this summit, or apex, the flow of water is directed to three separate oceans; meltwaters from tha Athabasca and Dome Glaciers flow northward and drain into the Arctic Ocean; the Saskatchewan Glacier, on the south side of Mount Athabasca in Banff Park, feeds the Saskatchewan River and drains into the Atlantic Ocean via Hudson Bay; all water flowing from the western side of the Great Divide drain into the Pacific Ocean.

The Athabasca Glacier, having formed at its toe the Sunwapta Lake, gives birth to the Sunwapta River, flowing north beside the Icefield Parkway. For the next several kilometres, bighorn sheep are to be observed near and/or on the roadway.

Passing Tangle Falls, the Stutfield Glacier is seen at the north end of the Columbia Icefield. This Glacier seems to hang between Mount Kitchener and Stutfield Peak.

At the Sunwapta Falls Junction, a short road gives access to view the Sunwapta Falls, where the river tumbles 600 meters to enter the mighty Athabasca River. From here a hiking trail heads southwest toward Fortress Lake. There is the Sunwapta Bungalow Camp at the parkway junction.

Just slightly north, on the east side of the parkway is an access to three small lakes; Buck Lake is the first, then Honeymoon Lake, and Osprey Lake behind it. This viewpoint across the wide Athabasca Valley offers sight to several spine-tingling summits. There is pyramid-shaped Mount Christie (3103 m), and Brussels Peak (3161 m) directly behind it, to the west; to the southwest, beside the Athabasca River is the glacial-covered Catacombs (3292 m); to the east is the reddish cliffs of Mount Kerkeslin (2984 m), upon which mountain goats may frequently be observed; far to the northwest is a first glimpse of the great Mount Edith Cavell.

The junction with the 93A Highway — a 23 km drive — gives access to the Athabasca Falls, where one witnesses the entire volume of the Athabasca River to drop turbulently into a narrow canyon before continuing its journey to the Arctic Ocean; past Leach Lake to Moab Lake Road, leading to the Athabasca Pass; a superb view of the majestic Mount Edith Cavell (3363 m) and the Angel Glacier; and a secondary road to Jasper's Marmot

Basin Ski Area. A trail west from Marmot (2608 m) leads to the Amethyst Lakes on the Great Divide.

Staying with the parkway, rather than venturing the 93A, you pass Horseshoe Lake and Mount Hardisty (2701 m) to the east; then the trail east over the Shovel Pass to the Maligne River; north of Shovel Pass is the trail to the beautiful Valley-of-the-Five-Lakes — meadows of wildflowers, pine and aspen forests housing many bird species, and perhaps a moose wading in the lakes.

Just before the Icefields Parkway meets the Yellowhead Highway, there are two junctions. Whistlers Road, to the right, toward Whistlers Summit, leads to the Whistlers Sky Tram, offering a panoramic view of Jasper townsite, and the surrounding mountains, lakes and rivers. Another junction to the left leads to Old Fort Point and the southeast side of Lac Beauvert.

Jasper townsite is situated in the wide valley of the Athabasca River, between where the Miette and Maligne rivers flow into it; and also it is where the Icefields Parkway meets the Yellowhead Highway, which leads east to Edmonton and west to Mount Robson Provincial Park via the Yellowhead Pass. Jasper found its identity in 1913, six years after the park was reserved.

Fitzhugh, the name of its former life, was conceived when the Grand Trunk Railway pushed through the Rockies in 1911. Another railway, the Canadian Northern, built in 1915, consolidated with the former in 1916. Now as one, the Canadian National Railway set to building the first tourist accommodation in the area; Jasper Park Lodge, on the shore of Lac Beauvert, one of many beautiful lakes in the town's immediate vicinity. Today's Jasper shelters some 3,000 inhabitants, and offers all the comforts of home to her visitors.

Jasper National Park stretches for better than 100 km from the townsite to its northernmost boundary, but the only means of experiencing this vast wilderness is by travelling afoot or on horseback.

An intricate system of hiking trails has been developed in the area, giving access to the numerous lakes just north of town. A road leads to the largest; lakes Patricia and Pyramid are shining at the foot of Pyramid Mountain (2766 m).

The Maligne Lake Road, intersecting the Yellowhead Highway 5 km west of Jasper, leads to Maligne Lake — one of the Canadian Rockies' most beautiful and famous attractions. But first, you must witness Maligne Canyon and Medicine Lake, two other amazingly wonderful features of the drive through the valley between the Maligne and Queen Elizabeth Ranges.

The labouring waters of the Maligne River erode the easily soluble limestone, to carve the deep, narrow gorges of the Maligne Canyon.

To the geologist, Medicine Lake is a phenomenon; to the Indians, the lake is truly "magic." The Maligne River enters the lake from the south, but there is no visible outlet to the lake. Medicine Lake appears perfectly normal when the water level is high during the summer months, but then becomes nearly bone-dry by late fall. Scientists believe the lake seeps into underground caves and travels thusly to the Maligne Canyon.

Maligne Lake — what may honestly be said of its indescribable beauty, of its dazzling colour, of the glaciers hovering the sheer cliffs and dense forests which envelop its narrow shoreline? Brazeau's Glacier (3470 m) gives the lake its life.

Westward along the Yellowhead Highway, toward the east gate of Jasper National Park, the road actually straddles two expansive lakes; Jasper Lake to the north and Talbot Lake to the south.

Roche Miette (2316 m), due west, tells you the park gate is near. Before leaving, however, there is a short drive south to the Roche Miette Hot Springs. Here, at the foot of Utopia (2563 m), one may bathe in the sulphur mineral springs — the warmest known in the Rockies. The lodge nearby offers delicious meals and comfortable accommodations. Once refreshed, hiking trails into countless kilometres of rugged backcountry await your enthusiasm.

Tents and recreational vehicles are accommodated from either May or June until mid-September at Honeymoon Lake, Jonas Creek, Snarling River, Wabasso, Wapiti, Whistlers and Wilcox Creek.

Tents only at Columbia Icefields, Miette Hot Springs, Marmot Meadows, Mount Kerkeslin, Ranger Creek and Whirlpool.

Wapititi also provides winter camping.

For information, contact The Superintendent, Jasper National Park, Box 10, Jasper, Alberta TOE 10E, Telephone (403) 852-4401.

Ice Fields Snow Coach

opposite: The Columbia Ice Fields

Mount Edith Cavell

Angel Glacier

Medicine Lake (Summer)

Medicine Lake (Autumn)

Jasper Tramway

Maligne Lake

KOOTENAY NATIONAL PARK

The friendly Kootenay Indians guided David Thompson in 1806 through their land which, with construction of the Banff-Windermere Highway in 1920, became the 1378 sq, km reserve of Kootenay National Park. The park is physically within British Columbia. Yoho borders it to the northwest and Banff, via the Great Divide, to the north-northeast.

It is from an enchanting storybook that we travel through in Kootenay Park. On either side of you, forests of pine, spruce and fir huddle closely to the roadside, where deer, elk, coyotes and bears are often seen; rivers are rushing and racing beside you, and all around the rocky mountains reach for the sky.

From Banff Park, over the Great Divide via Vermilion Pass (1651 m), one views what at first glance appears to be a grey, dismal landscape. In 1968, lightning caused an enormous 6,000 acre forest fire.

The trail to Stanley Glacier, south of Storm Mountain (3161 m), takes you through the Vermilion Burn where nature is busily creating a new forest from the old. Fireweed and Lodgepole Pine are spreading like wildfire! Stanley Glacier itself is a remarkable close-up observation of glacial activity.

The highway traces the Vermilion River for 60 km. It then follows the Kootenay River 25 km. From Sinclair Pass (1486 m), the highway is accompanied by Sinclair Creek as far as Radium Hot Springs.

An information bureau is situated at the junction to the Marble Canyon nature trail. Marble Canyon, where torrent glacial waters erode limestone to depths of 60 metres, is so named due to deposits of white marble visible throughout the area. The trail leads to Kaufmann Lake.

A trail south of Marble Canyon leads to the Paint Pots. These are pools of red and yellow ochre clay. Indians used the "paints" to colour their bodies, weapons and teepees.

At the Vermilion River Crossing is a picnic area and lodge. A trail to the west along Verendrye Creek leads to the foot of Mount Verendrye (3086 m).

Everywhere along the Banff-Windermere Highway one may discover numerous creeks flowing into the large rivers.

At the McLeod Meadows, the geological features of Kootenay Park begin to change. As the highway is directed away from the main ranges of the Rockies, the mountains are noticeably less tall or rugged. Now, also, fir trees become more abundant than the Pines of the subalpine forest.

From McLeod Meadows there several short, interesting hikes. Dog Lake is to the east, below Mount Harkin (2981 m) of the Mitchell Range. In the west is the Brisco Range and a trail to Nixon Lake. A fire road runs parallel to the highway on its east side and gives easy access to the Kootenay River.

Soon the Kootenay River will take a turn for the woods as the Banff-Windermere Highway swings westward and climbs through the dense forest to the Sinclair Pass (1486 m).

Lovely little Olive Lake appears just before Sinclair Creek tumbles rapidly past Kimpton Creek and Redstreak Creek, and into Sinclair Canyon, south of Radium Hot

Mount Stanley

Vermilion Pass Burn

Springs. Coming into Radium Hot Springs, the narrow highway squeezes between the "Iron Gates" — tall, reddish cliffs of eroded limestone and dolomite.

The Radium Hot Springs are so named because, compared to the other hot mineral springs in the Canadian Rockies, they are quite radioactive — though of a supposedly harmless degree.

From the hot springs to the west gate of Kootenay Park, a stretch of road less than 2 km long, you are offered the convenience of several lodgings, restaurants and shops. For further information, camping and fishing permits you will also find the Parks Canada Administration Centre.

Tents and recreational vehicles are accommodated at three areas: Marble Canyon, McLeod Meadows and Redstreak. These are open from either May or June until September.

Crook's Meadow is open until October, but only provides group tenting facilities.

The Dolly Varden picnic area has winter camping.

For more information, contact The Superintendent, Kootenay National Park, Box 220, Radium Hot Springs, British Columbia VOA 1MO. Telephone (604) 347-9615.

Eda Preznel

Mount Fay

Fay Hut

Numa Mountain

Cross-Country Skiing, Mt. Assiniboine in background.

Lake O'Hara

McArthur Lake

YOHO NATIONAL PARK

The Trans-Canada Highway and its parallel companion, the Canadian Pacific Railway, pierces through the heart of these 1313 sq. km of "awesome" wilderness. Awesome? "Yoho!", say the Cree.

Yoho, like Kootenay, is physically within the province of British Columbia. Its eastern boundary is the Great Divide, separating it with Banff National Park and with Alberta. To the southeast of Yoho is the boundary with Kootenay National Park.

Unlike Banff and Jasper Parks, Yoho hasn't the network of paved roadways to deliver one vis-a-vis with the many scenic places. One must, therefore, hike into the back country, should one desire of this park to reveal itself as truly "yoho."

The Kicking Horse Pass through the Great Divide — chosen in 1880 as the route for the railroad — makes the long descent to the valley below. Passing Sink Lake and the junction with the Bow Valley Parkway, you arrive at Wapta Lake, source of the Kicking Horse River. The river flows westward alongside the railroad and the highway, into the Columbia River and, eventually, the Pacific Ocean.

From Wapta Lodge is a panoramic view of peaks. To the north is Ogden (2684 m), Paget (2566 m) and Bosworth (2772 m). A short hike northward leads to Sherbrooke Lake; beyond here is Niles (2972 m) and Daly (3152 m), part of the massive Waputik Icefield. Looking south from Wapta Lake is Narao Peak (2913 m) to the left; Vanguard (2465 m), Cathedral Mountain (3189 m) and Cathedral Crags (3073 m) are to the right of the valley leading to Lake O'Hara.

Private vehicles are not allowed to travel the 13 km fire road into the Lake O'Hara area. One must hike from the parking lot or reserve a seat on the bus; reservations are made through the information centres in Field or Banff. The network of trails in the Lake O'Hara area is perhaps the best in the Canadian Rockies.

From Lake O'Hara Lodge and the Alpine Meadows campground one begins a wilderness adventure of colourful meadows and crystal clear lakes. Wildflowers, birds and wildlife abound this magic landscape. To the northwest, toward Cathedral Mountain, are three lakes: Linda, Vera and Cathedral below Mount Odaray (3103 m). Lake Oesa and Mount Yukness (2847 m) are east of Lake O'Hara. To the south, the McArthur Trail Pass junctions with the Ottertail fire road and heads southwest to Ottertail Falls on the Kootenay border. South of here tower the highest peaks in Yoho Park; Goodsir (3562 m), South Tower (3562 m) and North Tower (3525 m).

From Wapta Lake, the Trans-Canada Highway continues to descend toward the town of Field, passing a viewpoint for the Spiral Tunnels. The tunnels were constructed in 1909 to reduce the dangerously steep grade of the Canadian Pacific Railway. This viewpoint also reveals the Yoho Valley to the north.

The paved roadway up the Yoho Valley offers many magnificent scenes. Travelling right of Mt. Fields (2638 m), you witness the Meeting-of-the-Waters of the Yoho and Kicking Horse Rivers. The 13 km drive follows the Yoho River beneath Wapta Mountain (2779 m), past the youth hostel and the trail to Yoho Lake, and ends at the highest waterfall in Canada — Takakkaw Falls (380 m). A trail north from the campground heads toward Yoho Glacier (2760 m) of the Wapta Icefield, source of the Yoho River. Along this trail are seen two other falls, somewhat smaller yet just as spectacular. Laughing Falls and Twin Falls, where there is a Lodge.

Field townsite has nowadays little to do with the tourist industry, although it remains to serve as the Parks Canada's administration centre for Yoho National Park. Field — named after Cyrus Field, promoter of the Trans-Atlantic cable — is situated below the cliffs of Mount Stephen (3199 m). The village is now merely a division point on the Canadian Pacific Railway, though back in 1886, when the CPR built their first hotel in the Rockies (Mount Stephen House), Field was the hub of tourism.

Another famous attraction to Yoho Park is Emerald Lake. An 8 km paved roadway head north from the Trans-Canada, just west of Field. Arriving at the Lodge, you simply behold a dazzling blue-green gem — an emerald lake — surrounded with mountains. To the south, Mount Burgess (2583 m); to the east Wapta Mountain, where a trail leads to the backside of the President Range, which faces Emerald Lake to the north. Southwest of the lake is Hamilton Falls, the Hamilton Lake is a short hike to the northwest, below Emerald Peak (2543 m).

The Trans-Canada Highway, from the Emerald Lake junction, takes to the southwest and follows the Kicking Horse River between two mountain ranges. The Van Horne Range is to the north, the Ottertail Range to the south.

Before leaving Yoho through the west gate, where the highway swings due-west, there are three short, secondary roads. The first, to the south, passes a campground and ends in a parking lot, where a steep, 3 km trail climbs between Chancellor Peak (3280 m) and Mount Vaux (3320 m). Here stand the glacial and wind sculpted Leanchoil Hoodoos.

The second road heads north after you cross the Kicking Horse River Bridge. 3 km along the old road is the Chancellor Peak Campground and the commencement of some very long backcountry hiking.

The next adventure is to exit onto the southbound road leading to the Wapta Falls trail. The short hike from the parking lot takes you to the largest waterfall in Yoho National Park. A splendid view of the Ottertail Range may be seen from this boundary with the province of British Columbia.

Tents and recreational vehicles may find accommodation from May or June until September or October at the following areas: Chancellor Peak, Hoodoo Creek, Kicking Horse, Ottertail Camp. Lake O'Hara and Takakkaw Falls provide for tents only.
There is winter camping available at Finn Creek.

More information may be had from The Superintendent, Yoho National Park, Box 99, Field, British Columbia VOA 1GO. Telephone (604) 343-6324.

Twin Falls

Emerald Lake

Natural Bridge

opposite: Takakkaw Falls

Emerald Lake

Wapta Falls

opposite: Lake O'Hara

Waterton Lakes

Carthew Lake

WATERTON LAKES NATIONAL PARK

Established in 1895 with 54 sq. miles, the land known to the Indians as Omokisikimi ("beautiful waters") was then named Kootenay Forest Park. In 1911 the name was changed to Waterton Lakes National Park, in honour of the English naturalist, Charles Waterton. Even today, of 525 sq. km, it is the smallest of the parks, yet referred to by some as the loveliest reserve in the Canadian Rockies. And I can somehow see why....

Though it hasn't the abundance of glaciers and waterfalls seen in the northern Rockies, and though it has the highest level of precipitation in Alberta, it does have nearly the highest temperatures in the province! And the plentiful rains, together with the warm summer season, cause unique botanical conditions. Where the prairies meet the mountains is a floral wealth which makes Waterton famous, for here grow wildflowers and rare plants not to be discovered elsewhere in the province.

The human factor likewise enhances the charm and serenity of Waterton Lakes. It is known that many people visiting Waterton Park stay for entire seasons; there is not so much weekend traffic as we have at Banff. This, I believe, dispels any vanity which may more easily possess the other parks.

John George "Kootenai" Brown, a scholar at Eton and Oxford, was the first white settler in the area. It was 1865 when he found his true home. When the park was originally designated, Kootenai Brown became its first warden and, later, Acting Superintendent. He was buried on the shore of Lower Waterton Lake.

The park is entered by automobile from the north, via Pincher Creek, or from the east, via Cardston. The two roads junction near the park gates; travelling south, passing Lower Waterton Lake and Lonesome Lake, one arrives at the townsite — Waterton Park.

Comfortably situated at Emerald Bay, between Upper and Middle Waterton Lakes, is the town's centrepiece — the Prince of Wales Hotel, built by the Great Northern Railway; ironically, though, no railroad enters Waterton Park. There are other accommodations, and restaurants, and shops. Parks Canada issues fishing licenses and any information at the Information Centre. The view from the townsite is spectacular; to the south is the "beautiful waters", to the north is Mount Crandell (2831 m). Near the townsite, for your pleasure, is a golf course.

Southeast of the town, across the Upper Lake one sees Vimy Peak (2385 m). Hiking to the summit offers a breathtaking panorama of many lakes, mountains and prairie. Farther east is Sofa Mountain (2519 m), the source of Sofa Creek, which flows into the Lower Lake. Beyond here are the foothills, leading to the Belly River. Hiking the riverside northward one passes through the Blood Indian Reserve; or southward into Glacier National Park.

The Akamina Highway leads to Akamina Pass in the southwest. Here the Great Divide draws the park boundaries; British Columbia is to the west and the United States to the south. At the end of this road is Cameron Lake; behind it rises the Forum Peak (2414 m).

The Blakiston Valley to the northwest is the main valley in the park. The Blakiston Creek flows into the Dardanelles, between the Lower and Middle lakes. From this valley one may behold a wonderful view of Mount Blakiston (2922 m) and Mount Anderson (2651 m). North of Mount Anderson is the Bauerman Brook. It flows through Red Rock Canyon, where great deposits of red shale are discovered, before entering Blakiston Creek.

Should hiking become tiresome, climb aboard the passenger boat and cruise the Upper lake. The boat travels southward; Mount Richards (2392 m) rises to the west, Mount Boswell to the east. The two peaks, and a swath cut through the forest on either side of the lake, form the boundary of the international peace park.

Tents and recreational vehicles are accommodated at the park's townsite, Crandell Mountain and Belly River.

There is winter camping at the Pass Creek picnic area.

Waterton has many primitive campsites: Alderson Lake, Bertha Bay, Bertha Lake, Boundary Bay, Crandell Lake, Crypt Lake, Crypt Landing, Goat Lake, Lineham Lakes, Lone Lake, Rowe Basin, Snowshow, Twin Lake and Wishbone.

For further information, contact The Superintendent, Waterton Lakes National Park, Alberta TOK 2NO. Telephone (403) 859-2262.

The Banff Springs Hotel and Bow Valley